CW01017665

Barley

Life as a
Facility Dog Puppy

Written by Margot Bennett

with help from Barley

FETCH PRESS PUBLISHING

For permission requests, email tailsofdogswhohelp@gmail.com

Story and photography by Margot Bennett
Cover photo by Life's Highlights
Duke Puppy Kindergarten photos by Jared Lazarus and program
Chapter 2 "Flight of the Cuddles" courtesy of Charlotte Douglas International Airport
Photo modifications created by Sarah Rose Bischoff and Photo Lab
Cover design by Flames Creations
Chapter 10 team training and graduation photos by Canine Companions®
Book design by Sarah E. Holroyd (https://sleepingcatbooks.com)

Barley, Life as a Facility Dog Puppy/Margot Bennett — 1st ed.
Published
LCCN: 2024906558
Hardcover ISBN: 979-8-9902174-0-9
Paperback ISBN: 979-8-9902174-1-6
Ebook ISBN: 979-8-9902174-2-3

Produced in the United States of America

This book is dedicated to all those involved in the journey to becoming a service dog–breeder caretakers, volunteer puppy raisers, trainers, donors, administration staff and, of course, the graduates of Canine Companions®. Graduates are provided their service dogs at no cost thanks to all those involved in the puppy raising experience. Canine Companions® puppies are loved and cared for from before they are even born, until they have passed over the rainbow bridge.

I hope you enjoy the journey of one of these amazing dogs, Barley.

Proceeds from *Barley, Life as a Facility Dog Puppy* are donated to Canine Companions® to assist in providing training for present and future service dogs.

Other books by Margot Bennett

Tails Of Dogs Who Help Series
Brisco, Life as a Therapy Dog, Book 1
Ely, Life as a Service Dog Puppy, Book 2
Rocky, Life as a Guide Dog Puppy, Book 3

Introduction

Hello! My name is Barley and I am a yellow Labrador Retriever. I am a Facility Dog, which is a special type of assistance dog. There are many different kinds of assistance dogs such as service dogs, facility dogs and guide dogs, who help people who can't see.

I work in a courthouse. When children have to come to court and talk to all the grownups, that's where I come in!

My job is to:

- ❤ Snuggle with kids
- ❤ Lay quietly in a hidden spot
- ❤ Lend a paw so kids speak up

Do you have a favorite stuffed animal or blanket that you squeeze tight when you're scared or worried? I help just like that blanket does. Being with me gives a child the confidence to use their voice in court.

I always leave behind white strands of fur from my heart for the kids to carry with them.

Becoming a facility dog was not easy. It took a long time to learn everything I needed to be able to work with a woman named Kelsey.

Come along as I tell you my story!

Chapter 1
Barley and the B's

I was born in California on May 9, 2020 with nine brothers and sisters, all with names that began with the letter "B." We were all born into an elite non-profit organization called Canine Companions®.

This is our dad, Canine Companions® dog Colt.

Isn't he handsome? When I grow up, I hope I'm handsome like my dad.

This is our mom, Canine Companions® dog Clementine.

Clementine is *actually* a word for the color orange, but our mom is as dark as the night sky.

My mom and dad are both labradors. Labradors can have yellow, black, and sometimes even brown puppies! Humans call brown Labradors "chocolate." No matter what color, we are all loved and cared for from the very first day.

The Litter of B Puppies

Right after we were first born, the caretakers at Canine Companions® wrapped a different colored ribbon on each one of us.

Each color told the story of what order we were born in.

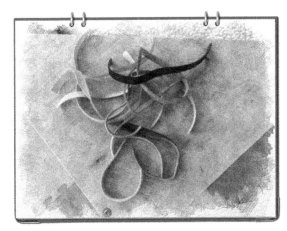

These ribbons also helped our caretakers tell us apart. This was hard to do when we were really little.

This is me! I was smaller than a piece of toast!

When we were first born, our favorite thing to do was squish ourselves together. We were a family and loved being snuggled up together.

Ten puppies squished together equals one impressive pile of cuteness!

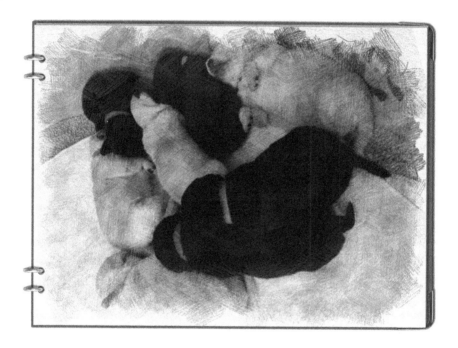

I wore a brown ribbon for being the sixth puppy born into our family of ten.

Can you tell which one is me?

Playing is Learning

After several weeks we could see more clearly, and our tiny bodies filled out into round balls of fur and wrinkles. We began to explore our play area and found some fun stuff:

- Toys that crinkled
- Things for chewing
- Squeaky soft caterpillars

All these different toys made learning fun.

Of course there were also pee pads for...you know...

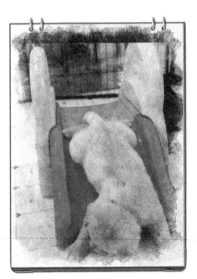

Sometimes I had so much fun that I wore myself out right in the middle of playtime.

Zzzz... I could sleep just about anywhere.

Sounds, Strokes, and Socks

As my littermates and I romped around, our caretakers played sounds to help introduce the real world to us. Loud beeps, thunderclaps, and soft music echoed around us.

At mealtime though? The only sound that could be heard for miles was the slurping of ten tiny tongues licking the bowls clean.

Every so often, I was picked up and cuddled. Hands softly stroked me from my ears down to my itty-bitty toenails. Fingers gently massaged my teeth and gums.

Once, I heard soft whispering in my ear.

"Aww, Barley, you have an angel's kiss on your head! You are *really* meant to be an amazing service dog one day."

The angel's kiss is a brown circle spot on Barley's head. It's called a *birthmark.*

I didn't know what a service dog was then. I just knew that I felt all warm and fuzzy being close to my caretakers. My little button nose rested right on top of some stinky socks.

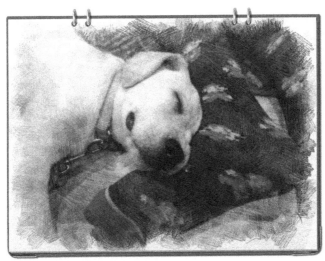

I fell asleep dreaming about mountains of kibble.
Who will I cuddle with tomorrow?

Chapter 2
Barley's New Home

O ne day it became clear something was happening. We were each given a bath and brushed until our fur was soft as silk. Our nails were clipped and our teeth brushed until they sparkled.

Meanwhile on the other side of the country, someone called a puppy raiser was also preparing—for ME! Weeks were spent reading about how to care for me and buying things I needed like toys, a soft bed, a toothbrush, and of course—food!

My caretakers tucked me into my travel kennel with a kiss, a hug, and a whisper, "You can do this, Barley!"

Questions danced in my head as we drove away. My heart filled with excitement.

- ♥ What will I learn?
- ♥ Will I meet new friends?
- ♥ Who will I cuddle with?

After my friends and I were settled on the airplane, a very kind and dedicated pilot flew us from California to North Carolina. Imagine, 14 future service dog puppies—from all different litters—on this one, special plane.

We called ourselves the Flight of the Cuddles!

Close your eyes and imagine the sounds of 14 puppies. What does it sound like to you?!

My TWO Puppy Raisers!

I had taken four puppy naps and missed breakfast by the time we landed. My tummy rumbled loudly as I was carried to a car for the next step of my adventure.

Umm, when's dinner?

I drooled a little thinking about my next meal.

I fell asleep, again, before the car had even pulled out of the airport. *Seriously?*

> An 8-week-old puppy needs 18-20 hours of sleep in a 24-hour period.

Then the door to my crate squeaked open and I woke up, peeking at the young woman looking at me.

Her gentle hands lifted me up into her arms and long hair tickled my nose.

"Hi, Barley. I'm Lizzie," she whispered. She softly rubbed the folds of skin on my puppy cheeks. She wrinkled her nose and giggled.

"You need a bath."

She carried me inside and lowered me into a tub with warm water. My paws slipped a little and she held me tight so I didn't fall on my bottom while she scrubbed me with shampoo.

"There you go, Barley," she whispered, wrapping a soft, warm towel around me and carrying me into another room.

"He's all nice and clean, Mom," she said, lowering me into someone's lap.

Mom? I glanced up and saw my *second* puppy raiser, Margot. *I have a mommy/ daughter team as my puppy raisers?*

I cuddled upside down with my second puppy raiser, my heart full.

Two puppy raisers means two times the snuggles!

More 'B's' in the House

I sniffed the air around me. Something smelled familiar–a delicious combination of chicken breath and dog fur. *Wait. More dogs?*

Suddenly there he was: a large, majestical yellow dog. He whispered to me, "*Hi Barley, I'm Brisco, your big brother.*"

I nudged him to play with me—"*Zoomies?*" I asked. We ran with each other back and forth, like the speed of light, then lay down, exhausted.

"*You may be little now but you are going to do big things someday, Barley,*" Brisco whispered.

My tail thumped a little with his confidence in me. Then he told me he did big things, too, and that one of my puppy raisers wrote a book about him.

Wow! Will my life be worthy of a book someday?

Exploring His New Home

Every morning, I woke up as arms lifted me out of the kennel and wrapped me in a hug. *Yay! Is it breakfast time already?* No, there was something I needed to do as soon as I came out of the kennel.

Can you guess the first thing I did every morning?

Before I had even eaten breakfast?

I used the bathroom of course! My puppy raisers called it **Hurry.**

During those first days, I even sniffed out a *different* dog, Aspen. When I first noticed her, she seemed so peaceful... I didn't want to disturb her. *Watch out, I'm coming in for my puppy nap!*

Aspen didn't even wake up as I snuck over to her. I nestled my nose into her snowy-white belly and fell asleep. When I woke up, she was gone. Unfolding my legs to search for her, I noticed something white and fluffy on the rug.

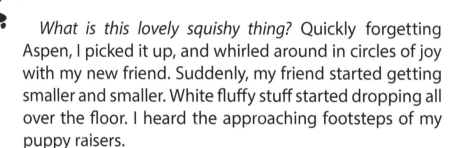

What is this lovely squishy thing? Quickly forgetting Aspen, I picked it up, and whirled around in circles of joy with my new friend. Suddenly, my friend started getting smaller and smaller. White fluffy stuff started dropping all over the floor. I heard the approaching footsteps of my puppy raisers.

"Oh, Barley," they said. I could feel the disappointment in their voices. I looked back at the trail of fluff and my heart sank.

Oops! Did I do something wrong? I tucked my tail in a little. I felt uncertain.

Lizzie sat on the floor and pulled me into her lap. While she rubbed my ears, she whispered, "It's okay, Barley. We should have been watching you. You're just a puppy and didn't know."

Phew! I felt relieved I was not in trouble.

I relaxed into a corner for my 10th nap that day.

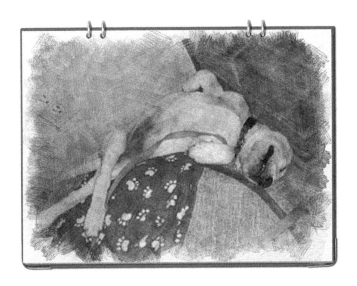

I could make myself fit anywhere.

Where is your favorite place to curl up for a nap?

Chapter 3
Barley Begins His Adventures

After a few weeks, my puppy raisers began teaching me skills. Each time I learned a skill I was rewarded with a treat. *This was fun!*

I looked into their eyes and waited for what was next. *I'm listening! I'm listening!*

I learned skills like **Here, Down,** and **Stand** while we played games inside and outside.

I swished my tail vigorously every time I was praised and given some kibble.

For dinner, I had to be extra patient. I waited on a special mat as my bowl was filled. It wasn't easy! The smell of *every* piece of kibble drifted into my nose and it felt like I waited for hours. My drool dribbled onto the mat.

Kibble is taken out from their meals for training purposes.

Then, *the word* was spoken. **"Okay!"**

Now I can eat!

I quickly devoured my food. When all the food was gone, I licked the bowl clean.

What will I learn next to earn some treats?

Trying on the Tiny Vest

It was now time for my first adventure. Margot tucked me into my puppy seat in the car and we were on our way. When we arrived at the store, she carried me inside and gently placed me on the carpet.

I stood still and glanced around as Margot carefully watched me. I was a little nervous about why we were here. Then, I heard her say,

"**Dress**." She fed me treats to encourage me to push my head through an opening in a yellow vest. I felt something tighten under my belly as she buckled the strap of my vest. *Thump! Thump!* I wagged my tail as Margot smiled at me.

"This coat shows others you are learning to be a service dog," she explained. *A Service Dog?* I had heard that word before. *What does it mean?*

Barley's training vest reads *Future Service Dog.*

I sat quietly on the rug inside and looked at her. I could feel a cool breeze as people walked by me. I waited for Margot to tell me what to do.

Soon, I heard her say, "Barley, **Let's Go**." We walked up and down a few aisles in the store. When we left the store, I wagged my tail proudly.

My first visit to a store was a success!

Going Out in Public

At home, Margot and Lizzie began taking turns with me outside. Everything outside was brand new for me. *Ooh, what are those things swirling around?* I watched as leaves drifted to the ground.

Ooh! Let me catch just one!

As a leaf spun towards me, I pulled my legs together for the chase. Suddenly, I heard Lizzie's voice call, "Barley!"

I turned my head. *Sniff, sniff. Mmm, I smell kibble!*

I had to choose. Play with the leaf or get kibble? I didn't think about it very long.

Puppy raiser for the win!

Lizzie smiled and rewarded me with a treat as I sat in front of her.

Then, we began to practice in new places like the nearby town, a playground, and the library. Everywhere we went, there was so much going on!

Can you think of other things outside that might be fun for Barley?

At first, I watched everything from a distance.

- Watching cars and people from the sidewalk
- Listening as children squealed on the swings
- Watching doors mysteriously open and close-just by pushing a button!

I practiced walking next to her as she went shopping, too.

Ooh...are we going to fill the cart up with kibble?
Sadly, the cart didn't magically fill up with my yummy treats. But, Margot rewarded me with kibble as I walked calmly next to her.
This is even better.

Discovering Surfaces

Often, we practiced walking together on different surfaces.

I splashed through puddles and water soaked in between my toes.

Ack! I'm not sure I like this squishy feeling.

At home, I crossed the family room, and my feet sank into the carpet.

Ahhh, so soft.

Sometimes Lizzie walked me on sidewalks where my toes curled up over bumps.

Ooh, that feels squishy. I was a bit unsure about the ticklish feeling and didn't move. Lizzie encouraged me forward, treating me to one kibble after another.

Munching on my last kibble I, wondered—

Why do my puppy raisers have me try so many new things?

Why do you think it's important for service dogs to learn to walk on different surfaces?

As she continued walking, I pranced after her on to our next adventure.

Being with my puppy raisers made me so happy, my tail swished back and forth.
Of course, so does earning kibble.
I looked forward to the day I would find out what kind of hero I would be.

I really like to nap. Will that be a way to help someone?

Chapter 4
Barley Goes to Puppy Kindergarten

My puppy raisers lived near Duke University where there is a program *just* for special puppies like me. Students run tests with the puppies to learn how they think. Understanding this will help future service dogs be more successful.

I also went to puppy class with other dogs just like me. We all wore our yellow vests and practiced walking on ramps, climbing steps, and greeting each other politely.

The hours I spent at Duke and in classes were in addition to the hours I spent with my puppy raisers.

A future service dog will spend 4,000 hours learning!

My favorite hour is, of course, dinner.
But does it really last an hour?
What do YOU think?

Duke University

Every two weeks, I traveled to Duke University for testing at their Puppy Kindergarten. On the very first visit, my collar was taken off and wrapped with something magical to record all my activity.

This activity monitor will measure Barley's sleep patterns and play activity.

They called it an "activity monitor."

Will they discover any superpowers in me?

While I wore my new collar, students played fun games with me, some of which were:

- 💜 Smelling for hidden treats
- 💜 Investigating strange toys
- 💜 Watching hand signals for clues

The students wrote down everything about me.
I barked 11 times at Mr. Clapping Monkey. Did you write that down?

When we got back home, I climbed into my favorite snuggle basket.
I don't think I'm going to fit in here much longer.

My puppy raisers always take off my collar when I go into the kennel. But this special one needed to stay on so it could measure my sleep activity.

Will it measure how many leaves I chase in my dreams?

After eight weeks, I graduated from the Duke University Puppy Kindergarten Program in a big ceremony.
I even earned a diploma!
Of course, my puppy raisers took a picture of me.

Doesn't Barley look handsome?

Puppy Class

Becoming a service dog means learning with a teacher, too. My puppy raisers took me to puppy class where we practiced around people, noises, and other dogs.

"**Side**," said Margot. "*Go to her right side,*" whispered the yellow dog on my right.

"**Up**," she sang. "*Place front paws onto a low table,*" the black puppy whispered on my left.

"**Heel**!" cheered Lizzie.

I know this one! Glide to her left and look into her eyes.

27

All the puppies in my class paraded around the store, one after the other. Our tails swished happily as people watched. Everyone was smiling and pointing at us. We were all so well behaved.

Every day, puppy class always ended with the teacher taking a photo of us showing off our skills.

Here are three skills my classmates and I are showing off—

- ♥ **Jump**
- ♥ **Up**

and

- ♥ **Under**

Can you guess which one is me?

Whenever we came home from class, I was so tired! I just wanted to curl my spaghetti legs into the coziest, softest place I could find.

Sniff, sniff. I walked from room to room. *Where's Brisco?*

I found him on his pillow in the kitchen and snuggled up next to him. I had grown so much I could hardly fit on the pillow with him.

Brisco whispered to me, "*What was your favorite part of class today, Barley?*"

I didn't have to think about it very long. "*Treats, Brisco. Treats.*"

How do you like to relax after a school day?

Chapter 5
Barley Practices: Here, There, and Everywhere!

I had more confidence with each adventure we went on.

- ♥ Coffee shops
- ♥ Libraries
- ♥ Neighborhood walks

We turned left. We turned right. Sometimes we turned around and went back to where we came from!

"Good boy, Barley!" My puppy raisers cheered as they led me up and down stairs, onto sidewalks, and back and forth across streets. I was getting exercise and having fun!

One day, a car stopped as we were relaxing outside. The driver opened his window and called out. "Is your dog okay? Do you need help?" The man's voice sounded very worried.

I immediately looked at Margot. *Was something wrong?*

She smiled at me, rubbing my ears as she laughed. Nothing was wrong.

I was just enjoying my cradle time.

Appointments

Sometimes, Margot brought me with her to important appointments like the dentist. These appointments were different than going to stores and the library.

She packed my bed so that I had my own place to relax. It was important I settle quietly and not bother other people who were waiting, or be in the way.

Humming and whirring noises floated around the room, but they didn't bother me at all.

I've got my eye on you!

Every few minutes Margot reached down to pat my head and feed me some kibble.

This is cool—I'm getting treats for doing nothing!

As we left the building, she encouraged me with kibble to try **Up.** I followed where her hands guided the treat, and lifted my front paws onto a bar.

Ooh, this is hard! I had a hard time keeping my paws on the handle. I tried several times as Margot counted. "One... Two..."

Then, Margot excitedly said, "Yes! Release! Good boy!"

I thought as I got back down: *that was hard. I'm glad she only counted to two!*

What do you think Barley will use Up for?

32

Every week we visited the grocery store, which was filled with bright lights and yummy smells. When we went, Margot had me practice **Heel, Side,** and **Back**.

It was important that I learn not to be distracted by things around me:

- Children crying
- Grocery carts squeaking
- People passing us

One time, she had me practice **Under** the bakery table! It was hard to lay still with all the yummy smells on the shelf above me.

I wonder if people thought I was for sale for $2.99?

Training at Home

In addition to working on skills away from home, we practiced in our house, too. I lay next to my puppy raisers while they read on the couch and snuggled with them as they stretched on the floor.

One afternoon, I practiced a new skill called **Visit.** Margot encouraged me to place my head on her lap while she played the drums.

The rumbling sound made my ears flap.

Tee-hee, that tickles.

A Visit from a service dog can provide comfort.

Margot rubbed my head as she fed me some treats. *That was fun!*

If Margot needed me to stay in one place while she moved around the room, she told me "**Bed**." Sometimes I don't always get it right.

Laughter bubbled up from her as she saw my first attempt.

"Barley, you need your entire furry body up on your bed, not just your paw," she explained.

Oops, silly me.

I wiggled this way and that way until I was all the way on the mat.

Now can you see my Angel's kiss birthmark on my head?

Barley Learns to Speak

One time while practicing with Lizzie, I thought I saw a DOG on the pillow. *Is it real?* I backed up a little and turned to her.

Can you see that dog behind me?
Dogs shouldn't be on the furniture, right?

This is what Barley sees.

She ignored my silent plea and kneeled down. "Barley," she whispered. "It's time to teach you to **Speak**."

But wait! What about the DOG?

"**Speak**!" she said.

I looked at her and wagged my tail. I silently shared my concern again.

But the dog?

"You can do it, Barley. **Speak**!" This time I licked my lips and stuck out my tongue. "Yes, Barley, almost! **Speak**!" Lizzie fed me some kibble.

This time, I released a grumbling noise. Then a bark escaped. I was so surprised at hearing my own voice that my front paws hopped off the ground.

"Yes!" Lizzie hugged me and gave me a big sloppy kiss. "You did it!"

I knew I had learned how to **Speak**, but Lizzie still didn't understand my concern.

That *dog* was still on the pillow.

I walked up to the pillow and whispered to it— *You are NOT supposed to be on the furniture,* then I left the room.

We Are Out and About!

As I began to feel more confident around noises, Margot brought me with her to concerts at school. The auditorium was huge and filled with people—and noise. Lots of noise! We sat in the front row and listened to what she called "music."

Frankly, I didn't know what to call it.

I sat in front of Margot and stared at her while she listened to this *music.*

Wow, she seems fascinated with this noise. Why?

My puppy raisers also took turns walking me around town. I was as SLOW as molasses. Occasionally we'd stop at a bench and they'd say, "Barley, **Under.**"

Yay! I loved hiding down here. It was a whole different world for me to watch. I could spy squirrels, little feet and big feet, and sometimes even furry feet!

What would you see if you were hiding under a bench?

I even climbed the steps into a bus! I practiced my **Jump** skill to get up on the seat. Then I waited patiently for the word for me to get down—**Off.**

Every week, Margot took me with her to a thrift store where she worked. I lay on my bed while she sorted, ticketed, and stocked the bookshelves.

Honestly, it was a bit boring and I always fell asleep. When I started snoring, it got so loud *everyone* looked around and giggled.

"That noise is Barley, not me!" Margot told everyone as she laughed along with them. They smiled at me. My being there—snoring or not—made their day.

Some days I just couldn't hold it together. In the middle of shopping at the grocery store, I flopped upside down—right next to the bananas. Lizzie giggled at me.

"Oh Barley, it's time to stop practicing, isn't it?"

I rolled over and stood up, wiggling my entire body to show her how happy I was to hear that.

Even though we were not done shopping, she knew I needed to stop working. She led me to the car, and we drove home.

I hope we can play fetch when we get home!

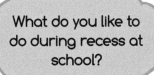

What do you like to do during recess at school?

Chapter 6
Adventures Far From Home

As the months passed, I continued visiting stores and restaurants to practice my skills. One day, Margot whispered to me, "Barley, we're going to meet someone really special today!"

Ooh, the creator of dog treats?

She sounded super excited as she chatted during the drive. When we got out of the car, there was a dog who looked just like me—except his puppy vest was blue.

I couldn't smell dog treats but the scent of my older puppy raiser was very strong in him. *Why does this dog smell like Margot?* He sat patiently next to a woman in a wheelchair as we waited for permission to say hi.

As we greeted each other politely, he whispered to me, *"I'm Ely, a service dog for the woman next to me."*

Ely? Where have I heard that name before?

Ely whispered back, *"Margot wrote a book about me, just like Brisco—she was MY puppy raiser, too!"*

I swished my tail. *Wow, I know two famous dogs!* No, wait.

They're not just dogs.

They are real dogs who help.

Just like I will someday!

I wonder what adventures Margot might write in a book about me?

Visiting the Beach

When I turned a year old, the days began getting longer, and the sun got hotter every day. It was time for a vacation! The entire family loaded into the car and drove to where I smelled salty air for miles.

On our first day, we all headed to the pool where Margot pointed and said, "Barley, **Bed**." I curled myself onto the mat to prepare for a nap when…

Wait a minute… Ooh, this is cold! What kind of bed is this?

My puppy raisers knew I needed a special cooling mat in the hot sun.

I lay in the coolest spot around, thankful for them taking such good care of me.

It's important to take care of your pets in any kind of extreme temperature.

As I drifted off to sleep, I listened to the squeals of the small humans as they leaped into the water. Cool drops splashed my fur. Somewhere around us, music played.

When my family returned to our room, everyone played games and chatted. I found myself a hiding spot.

I bet they can't see me here.

Can YOU see me?

Sometimes they took me to a place where they held sticks and hit little round balls. The balls would roll under tunnels, across bridges and even climb hills. Eventually they disappeared into a small hole in the ground.

As we walked from hole to hole, I continued to see this really mysterious creature. My puppy raisers called it a pig. When we got really close to it, they told me **Sit**. I wondered—*I know I'm supposed to sit until my puppy raiser releases me but...*

Who's going to tell this pig he can get up?
He's been sitting here since they started their game!

Every day as the sun was going down, we all took a walk along the beach. With each step, my paws sunk into thousands of grains of sand. One night as I walked next to the roaring water, I wanted to see what the vast ocean felt like.

I backed up and took a running leap into the water. *Whoa!*

As soon as I hopped into the seawater up to my belly, I knew I had made a mistake. I immediately turned around and ran the other way.

Dang! That water was cold!

Have you been in the ocean when it's really cold?

Barley Climbs the Mountains

ater in the summer, my family took me on a different kind of adventure. We took long hikes up to the top of the mountains. My toenails gripped onto massive rocks as we continued higher and higher.

Even though these vacations weren't as relaxing as the beach, I loved this new experience. I could see the world around me for miles.

I thanked Lizzie the best way I knew how.

Here, let me give you a big, sloppy kiss.
Sllllllurrrpppppppp.

Our time in the mountains was filled with new things to experience, too. There were creeks to wade in, trails filled with wood chips, and trees as tall as the sky. On a bridge we crossed, I thought—

Whoa! I'm higher than the treetops!

A sense of bravery came over me. I sat tall and proud while Lizzie snapped a picture of me.

"Look at you, so confident. Barley, **Here**!" As I walked to her left and sat down, she whispered to Margot—

"Mom, he's getting so big! I can't wait to see how he will help someone someday."

Have you ever walked on a really high bridge like Barley?

Me too! I wonder what I will do?"

49

Barley Meets Snow

Summer ended and the air started to turn colder. One morning when we were staying at a cabin in the woods, I heard all sorts of squealing and feet running around. Thinking everyone was getting breakfast ready *(because mealtime is #1 in my book)* I darted to the kitchen.

Aspen was plopped right in front of the door, so I joined her. I looked outside, then at her, then outside, then at her.

Why had the world outside turned white?

"Get ready, Barley," she whispered. *"This white stuff is going to turn your paws into icicles!"*

When Margot opened the door, we bolted. Boy, did I stop fast! *Brrr!* My paws sank into the white fluffy floor but *woof…*

I was chilled to the bone!

Zooming around this white fluffy stuff was fun but...

...it was so cold my *drool* turned into an icicle!

Can you see it?

I thought about all the things I had learned so far.

One minute passed by. *That's enough thinking, time to curl up back inside the warm house.*

I wondered as I trotted inside—*Have I learned everything I need to be somebody's helper?*

What would you teach Barley to help you with?

51

Chapter 7
Barley and Time at Home

Practicing my skills in the community was a big part of the time with my puppy raisers, but I was also a part of the family. I chased tennis balls in the backyard with Aspen, I nestled in the leaves while Margot planted flowers, and I took walks every morning to the bus stop.

On some days, I just enjoyed snuggling with Brisco on his favorite pillow.

It was so nice of him to share.

I had personal health care, played with my toys, and helped with schoolwork.

Yes, I helped with homework! Let me tell you more.

My Family Takes Care of Me

Every day I was learning skills to be a service dog. While I was learning, every day my puppy raisers were also taking care of ME! My puppy raisers took time every day to care for my health.

Did you know dogs have 18 nails on their paws?

A dog's nails can get long just like yours. Since we can't trim them ourselves, we depend on others—like my puppy raisers! They use a tool that files a dog's nails as it spins really fast.

Lizzie introduced me to the spinning tool first. It had a motor that was loud and scared me when she turned it on.

The first time, I stared at this strange, new tool in alarm.

When I felt the spinning tool gently buzz one toenail, I pulled my paw back.

"It's okay, Barley," Lizzie whispered as she shared a treat with me. "Just one toe today."

Day after day Lizzie brought out this buzzing tool to help me be comfortable with it. Soon, I was letting her file two or three nails at a time.

My puppy raisers took care of me in other ways, too. What I loved the most was was having my teeth brushed.

Yummm. My toothpaste tastes like chicken—what does yours taste like?

I could smell the chicken toothpaste from the other side of the house! As its scent wafted into my nose, I lay on my back and showed Lizzie my pearly white teeth.

I am ready!

Are my teeth twinkling brightly at you?

Shopping

One day, there was all sorts of excitement when my puppy raisers took me shopping. Lizzie kept disappearing into a little room as I waited under a table. Every time she came out the door, she looked different. It was like she was magically changing every time she vanished and then reappeared.

It was fascinating, but honestly? I was bored.

I guess clothes shopping isn't my thing.

Why do you think it's important for Barley to be content doing nothing?

Humans Have School Too

On school days, Lizzie and her brother Alex disappeared all around the house to work on their homework:

- Upstairs
- Downstairs
- Even on the couch!

I wanted to keep everyone company. Every time I wondered, *Who should I go with today?*

When Alex sat at his computer, I crawled into my kennel while *he* did all the brain work. Fractions and fancy words echoed from the computer. It was hard to keep up with everything he was learning and I faded quickly.

My contribution to his assignments was the loud rhythm of my snoring as I drifted into clouds full of tennis balls and yummy treats. When I woke up, he had put on his headphones.

Was my snoring that loud?

I lay quietly next to Lizzie as she worked silently on her own computer. She focused hard, listening to jumbly words that I couldn't understand.

I tried to be invisible so I didn't disturb her concentration. Every once in a while, she would lean against me and rest her arm on my back.

Do you think this will help with Barley's future role as a service dog?

"Barley," she said, "you make it so much easier to work on homework."

She DOES relax the longer I lay next to her, which makes me happy.

One day when the kids were in school, Margot drove with me to a place where she said she was going to 'vote.' I wasn't sure what that meant but it was really quiet in the big room.

I stood silently next to her as she did this *voting* thing.

Margot seemed really proud when someone took our picture together.

Happiness, being nervous, disappointment—I could sense lots of emotions with them. If I felt an extra hug was needed, I leaned into them to make sure they knew I was there.

I can really pick up what they are feeling. Like a detective! Will that be helpful to someone someday?

Chapter 8
Barley's Personality Shines

The weeks flew by—79 weeks to be exact! Each one had been filled with new experiences.
I even got to spend some time with my furry friends!

This is Weston, my pool buddy. We had sleepovers where we watched squirrels, chased each other around the yard, and even went swimming!

Can you guess how we like to swim? Doggie paddle of course!

Weston knew all the skills I did, so we also practiced them together. He was older than me and helped if I wasn't sure what to do.

I soon had my own puppy to play with!

Barley and the New Puppy

When a tiny black ball of fur came to stay with us for a few days, I greeted him right away.

Sniff. Sniff. You smell brand new.

The little puppy whispered to me that he was going to the Duke Puppy Kindergarten Program.

"Hey, that's where I went!" I shared about ALL the cool games we did and assured him he would have oodles of fun.

Since he was so little, he was fed THREE meals a day. I only got TWO.

Hmmm, I may go on Big Barley adventures, but I sure wish I could have Baby Barley meals.

My tummy rumbled as I watched him devour his extra bowl of kibble. Even Aspen was upset.

The Barley Smush

After being with my puppy raiser family for so long, I made up a new word for something I loved more than anything—I insisted on being as close to my puppy raisers as I could. I wanted to *smell* their emotions, *feel* their day, and *understand* their innermost thoughts.

My new word? SMUSH. I tasted it on my tongue. Perfect. The Barley Smush.

When I curled up next to them, I felt their heartbeat slow down and their bodies relax.

This is my purpose, I realized.

It's important for me to be right here with you! I whispered to them.

Barley Tries To Help

The closer I became to my puppy raisers, the more I began to feel the need to be near them. I stood over my puppy raisers as they lay on the rug.

Can I help you?

Do you need me?

I really didn't have any concept of space. They didn't seem to mind me being so close.

Oops! There goes a bit of drool. Sorry.

I attached myself like glue as they walked from room to room. Sometimes I put myself in a helping position...I thought.

Is this what a service dog might do?

"Oh, Barley," Margot said, looking down at me. "Are you trying to help?"

Yes, I am!

I'm helping, right?

"I'm sorry, but laying here is *not* helpful, Barley. I need to close the door, silly," she informed me. She pointed to my special mat and told me, "Barley, **Bed**."
I groaned heavily as I got up to move to my mat.

I sat quietly, patiently waiting for what to do next.

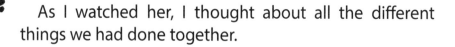

As I watched her, I thought about all the different things we had done together.

- Exploring many different places in my vest
- Learning 30 skills
- Having adventures in the sun, snow, and on mountaintops

My puppy raisers had helped me become the special dog that I am today. They whispered to me many times that I was very gentle, and the best cuddler ever.

Maybe being calm and snuggling was my special purpose.

Will that determine who will be my partner?

Chapter 9
Barley Goes to Professional Training

I began to feel something was changing. The air was filled with smells of excitement—and yet I sensed something else. It reminded me of when my siblings and I left on our first adventure.

Does this mean I am leaving soon for the next part of my journey?

The entire family gathered outside, where my puppy raisers told me, Aspen and Brisco to **Wait**. We whispered back and forth, watching as all sorts of goodies were placed into bowls.

"I smell vanilla ice cream," said Brisco.
"Peanut butter is there for SURE," exclaimed Aspen.
"Mmmm!" I sniffed. *"Bananas."*

"Banana splits for Barley!" My puppy raisers cheered for me as they raised the bowls and carried them over to us like we were royalty.

It was a celebration! *They're celebrating ME!*

I slurped my bowl until there was no more. Then, I padded over to snuggle with Alex. I sensed sadness in him.

As I lay with my friend, I wondered if this was the kind of place I was needed.

- *Do I bring Alex comfort?*
- *Does it help him when I snuggle in tight?*
- *Was my purpose to let little humans be close to me?*

I lay with Alex for a long time, counting the birds as they flew by. I felt his heartbeat next to mine. I shed magical fibers of love as we sat together.

It was time to travel to Orlando for Professional Training.

Barley Flies with his Puppy Raisers

We had to travel a long way to get to professional training. Again, that journey started on an airplane.

It was February 10, 2022, eighteen months after our adventure began. The entire family came with Margot and Lizzie to the airport. There were so many suitcases!

Did they pack one for me? I'm not going to miss dinner, am I?

I could feel sadness mixed with excitement as everyone said good-bye. I leaned into my puppy raisers to bring them comfort. This seemed to be a day filled with heavy emotions.

Then, it was time to be on our way.

As we walked through the airport, people rushed past us talking on their phones, carrying crying babies, and pulling suitcases.

Everyone is in such a hurry!

Speaking of **Hurry**…

We stopped in a special relief area for me to try to use the bathroom. I sniffed around and could smell all the other dogs that had been there before me. *No, thank you, no need to pee for me.*

Then, I boarded the plane with my puppy raisers and curled up on the floor in front of their seats. Lulled to sleep by the motion of our flight, I relaxed for the rest of our journey.

…and my snoring brought giggles to everyone on the plane.

Leash Handoff

It was dark when we arrived at our hotel room and Margot and Lizzie settled us into the room. I could smell several emotions floating around them like bubbles—sadness, excitement, and nervousness.

Then, I heard Lizzie say, "Barley, **Jump**."

Wait, she's inviting me onto the bed with her? There must be a special reason for this.

I hopped up onto a soft, warm spot next to Lizzie and snuggled in close. I let her wrap her arms around me and melted into her.

Dogs in training are not allowed on the furniture.

I whispered to her—*Thank you for all you have taught me. I know someone out there needs me more, but I will never forget my time with you.*

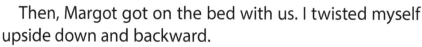

Then, Margot got on the bed with us. I twisted myself upside down and backward.

I can still make myself fit anywhere!

I felt her head rest on my belly.

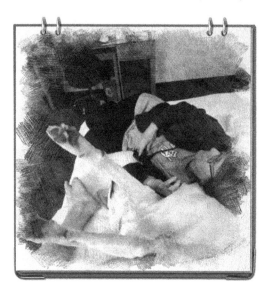

I whispered to her too—

*I'm going to use **Cradle** and **Lap** the most. Thank you for teaching me.*

I felt her heartbeat slow and her body relax. We all fell asleep together on our last night.

The next morning, we drove from the hotel to the Canine Companions® Professional Training Center. The air was thick and sticky with heat.

After we checked in, Lizzie said, "**Dress.**" I pushed my head through the blue training vest. I heard the familiar click as the vest was fastened under my belly.

The blue color of my new vest makes me feel so handsome! I wonder if I look like my dad?

Margot and Lizzie stepped back to look at me.

I looked back at them.

We sat together, snuggled,

took more pictures, and hugged some more.

Then, it was time to hand my leash over to the trainer.

This was it.

The trainer walked me into the training center and I turned around.

"You're going to do great, Barley!"

"Find your person!"

"We love you!"

My puppy raisers were both cheering for me.

I could see happy tears as they waved goodbye. I swished my tail a little slower. My heart beat a little faster and my stomach churned. *I'm nervous. Will I make new friends in training?*

Barley Adjusts to Professional Training

In professional training, there were other dogs learning new things, just like me. We shared toys and explored the playground together.

I even had a roommate—his name was Vertex!

Every night before we fell asleep, Vertex visited close to me and asked,

"What was your favorite thing today, Barley?"

"Mealtime, Vertex. Mealtime."

I always slurped the bowl clean after every bite.

My trainer worked with me and several other dogs—called a 'string.' We each took turns working with her and practicing the skills we already knew. Puppy raisers from all over the country had helped us prepare for this–and it showed!

We also had lots of time to play. My favorite playmate was a Canine Companions® Dog in Professional Training, Sparky. Sparky was fast and loved to play chase. We ran like the wind during our free time.

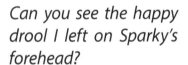

Can you see the happy drool I left on Sparky's forehead?

Every day, we were loaded up in a special van to go on field trips to practice and learn new skills. Over time, our trainer began putting several skills together to form a task. We heard familiar words mixed with the new ones.

When it was my turn, I heard my name first, followed by the task. Then another. Then another.

1. Barley, **Get**
2. Barley, **Lap**
3. Barley, **Drop**

Barley learned to pick up a phone, pencil, and a water bottle.

I did them all, one after another—even the new task I had just learned!

Remember how hard it was for me to learn **Up**? In training, I learned to use it with another skill, and was able to turn on a light switch!

One time, my trainer taught me a new task, and I fell in love with it. She encouraged me to climb *over* her lap and then lay down. She called it **Cover**.

I called it snuggling!

I walked back to the other dogs with a little strut of pride in my step. I had learned something so perfect for me. I knew right away what my favorite thing was that night when Vertex asked.

Cover!

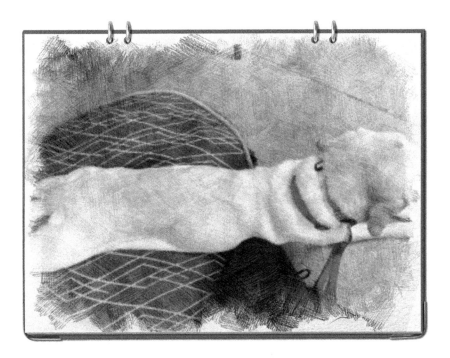

I lay across my bed and wondered.
How might I be able to use **Cover** *as a service dog?*

75

Chapter 10
Barley Finds His Forever Home

One morning we woke up to all sorts of activity around the training center. New people walked around with suitcases rolling behind them. The air was filled with the smell of excitement—and delicious food!

Six months had passed–180 days filled with learning, playtime, and field trips. It was now time for Team Training. People had traveled a long way to be matched with one of us as their future service dog.

Look at how amazing our team of dogs looked—we were ready to meet our future partners!

Can you guess which one is me?

During Team Training, I practiced with two people. Sometimes I walked next to a child in a wheelchair, proudly picking up something they had dropped. The rest of the time I spent getting to know a woman named Kelsey.

We were surrounded by people who did everything possible to help us do our best.

- ❤ "Thank you for bringing my water bottle," whispered the little boy.
- ❤ "Awww, you are such a soft, cuddly boy," said Kelsey.
- ❤ "Barley, **Tug**!" They both requested. I used my tug toy to open the door for them.

All the things I had learned from my breeder caretaker, my puppy raisers, and my trainers had led to this moment.

Who would it be?

Are you ready to meet Barley's partner?

Barley Finds His Match

After four days of working with my new friends, my trainer had made her decision. Today was the day I was going to be officially matched with my partner!

Will my forever person like my Barley Smush?

As all the dogs were led into our training room, I looked ahead and saw Kelsey. I peeked up at my trainer. My trainer nodded and encouraged me forward.

I swished my tail wildly as I trotted over to Kelsey. My heart was thumping with joy.

I sat in Kelsey's lap and watched as all the other teams were placed together.

She rubbed the special angel's kiss on my head and snuggled me close. She whispered all the things she loved about me.

I spent the next week with Kelsey learning how to help her. She whispered to me, "Barley, you're going to become special friends with the children I work with. Let's practice ways you can help them."

- **Lap** (to allow kids to pet me in their lap)
- **Jump** (to curl up on the couch in the lobby for snuggles)
- **Get** followed by **Give** (to pick up dropped items like pens and water bottles)

At this point, Barley had learned 40 skills.

At night, I was so exhausted, I could barely keep my head on the pillow.

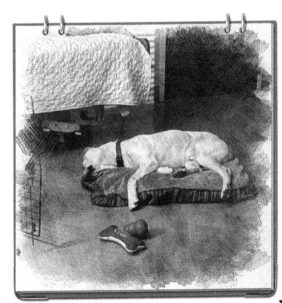

As my snoring echoed around our room, I thought I heard Kelsey giggling, but I was too tired to check.

Graduation

On our last day, my trainer woke me up early. She led me away from Kelsey's room and into the training room.

Wait! Why was Kelsey not coming with me?
Then, a familiar smell filled me with excitement. *Sniff. Sniff.* These weren't just *any* smells.
Wait…is it?? Really??

I galloped towards the smell of my childhood memories. I curled into the open arms of my puppy raisers. My tail swished with joy at seeing Margot and Lizzie again. They had come here to congratulate me and meet my new partner.

I was so excited to see them, my thoughts came tumbling out all at once—

- *Let me tell you about all I learned!*
- *I can't wait to introduce you to Kelsey. She says I'll be helping children when they're scared. I have a job!*
- *Everything you prepared me for is happening!*

I think I finally ran out of words!

Settling down, I lay with my head on Margot's lap and enjoyed our last few minutes together before the ceremony.

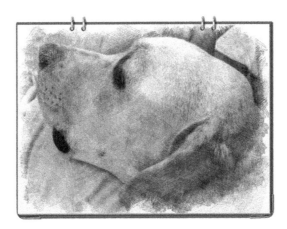

Then, it was time. All the dogs, puppy raisers, and graduates filed into the auditorium. The celebration of puppies coming into Professional Training, and older dogs graduating with their partners had begun.

As Margot and Lizzie sat with me during the ceremony, I dreamt about the friends I had made, the things I had learned, and all the people who had helped along the way.

My snoring echoed quietly as we all waited for our turn to walk up onto the stage. Suddenly, my name was called! Both of my puppy raisers walked with me up the stairs to my new partner, Kelsey.

I watched as they hugged.

A few tears slowly slid down their cheeks as everyone smiled and stood proudly together.

I was now a Facility Dog. Kelsey and I graduated as a team on August 12, 2022.

Barley: Courthouse Facility Dog

My home with Kelsey was meant to be from the very beginning. I could curl up on my very own bed, play fetch in the yard, and sleep all day if I wanted. Except, of course, when I was working.

I even shared my new home with three cats—Koji, Snow, and Calliope.

"Will you smush with me?" I whispered to them.

"Um, no," they meowed.

Sigh. I humphed and lay in the corner of the bed by myself.

When Kelsey brought me to work with her, I snuggled wherever I was needed. Even with toys and games to play with, the kids wanted to be with me more than anything else.

There were days that I snuggled with a child for the entire afternoon. When some of my favorite people walked by, I peeked up at them but stayed where I was...

...giving freely what I do best—love and comfort.

I could lay here for hours.

I melted into the hands that rubbed my ears and belly. Of course, my snoring brought out their giggles. My tail thumped in agreement that I was silly.

When children needed to talk about sad and scary things, I rested quietly in the witness box with them, where no one else could see me. I waited and watched to see if they needed me.

- ❤ *Do you need a **Visit**?*
- ❤ *I can put my paws on your **Lap** if you need me!*
- ❤ *I'm right here if you need to pet me!*

When we visited the Child Advocacy Center, Kelsey asked the children, "Do you want Barley to open the elevator door for you?"

Can you guess what skills Barley used to open the elevator door?

"Yes! Yes!" They squealed with excitement.

I swished my tail happily and showed the children my amazing elevator door skills.

Sometimes Kelsey and I went to special events that helped share about the Courthouse Facility Dog Program.

I am so handsome and dignified... don't you agree?

I sat patiently, oozing with charm, as I waited for snuggles.

Weeks went by and Kelsey was so impressed by how nothing bothered me. Loud noises, music blaring, and squeals of children couldn't could keep me from doing my job.

From the day I was born, and every step along the way, I learned to become the hard-working dog I am today. I didn't do this alone though. It took my amazing breeder caretaker, puppy raisers, and trainer to teach me during my journey.

My life before Kelsey.

Now, my heart is made up like a puzzle--complete with pieces of all those who helped me to become the dog who I am today.

A Facility Dog. A Dog with a job.

"Woof, the end!"

Note From the Author

Covid

Barley was with our family for nineteen months–July 2020 until February 2022. He began with us during the height of Covid. In the beginning, this didn't impact his training since he only needed to focus on learning good manners and getting to know us. That's why there are many pictures throughout the story of people in masks, and most activities take place outside or at home.

Over time, we were able to go out in public again and socialize Barley through interactions with people and noises. We're fortunate that our family is involved in various music programs, so Barley was able to come to concerts and hear handbells and marching bands. We also live in an active community which is near a train station and several businesses, which provided exposure to many sights and sounds.

Kelsey, Barley's partner, has said how important this has been for Barley, who is impressively unbothered by most loud noises. Where he works near downtown Tampa can be quite loud—police and fire sirens are a constant. There are times when voices are loud or kids cry. Barley doesn't even flinch.

Reunion

One of the most rewarding experiences of being a puppy raiser is keeping in touch with the graduate of a service dog you raised. And even better? Having a reunion!

We've had several reunions with Barley and took such pride in seeing him with Kelsey, his handler. There was a bit of confusion when he first saw us: he gave side glances to Kelsey as he took in our scent and familiarity.

If Barley had thought bubbles, they might have read:

- *Sniff, sniff—they smell like my puppy life!*
- *Wait, is it...my puppy raisers?*
- *What are they doing here??*

Nevermind! Barley Smush coming in!

His tail swished wildly as his body wiggled back and forth, and we leaned into the puppy love he poured into our reunion.

Until next time.

The circle of a puppy raiser life—Raise, Turn In, Let Go, Raise again.

Thank you for adding *Barley, Life as a Facility Dog Puppy* to your library. If you and your child enjoyed this story, please consider posting a thoughtful review on Amazon, Goodreads or other favorite book site. Your kindness will make a difference for others considering this book.

Proceeds from *Barley, Life as a Facility Dog Puppy* are donated to Canine Companions® to assist in providing training for present and future service dogs.

Did I catch your attention?

Canine Companion Facility Dogs can be trained to support in a variety of ways. They can also perform a variety of tasks. Let me tell you about all the different places where Facility Dogs can help!

Occupation, speech and physical therapy

Special Education settings

Child Life Specialists

Criminal justice placements

Facility Dogs provide unconditional love and attention to their clients and staff with whom they interact.

Canine Companions® Facility Dogs and follow-up services are free of charge.

Puppy Talk!

Puppy, Puppy, Puppy: Birth through 8 weeks

What is a Breeder Caretaker? Breeder Caretakers are volunteers who provide specially bred mom and dad dogs a healthy and happy home. When caring for a female who has a litter of puppies, these volunteers raise and socialize puppies per Canine Companions® early care protocols.

What is a "litter?" A litter refers to the number of puppies born at the same time by the same female dog. All the brothers and sisters make up a 'litter.' All Canine Companions® puppies born in the same litter have a name that begins with the same letter!

Birth order and collar color—Each puppy is given a different colored ribbon when they are born. Ribbon colors represent the order in which puppies are born, and help keep track of the puppies as they grow. They all look so much alike!

Puppy Raiser Time—8 weeks through 14-20 months

What is a Volunteer Puppy Raiser? Puppy raisers are volunteers who take a puppy into their home and provide love, care, training and socialization until it is time for professional training.

Why is it so important for a puppy to 'speak'? Barking can be a valuable tool to get help. If someone with a disability is home alone and happens to fall down or need other assistance, they could give their service dog the command to 'speak' to get the attention of someone nearby.

How long is a puppy with a volunteer puppy raiser? A puppy stays with their puppy raiser anywhere from 14–20 months.

Training Tools

What is the purpose of the training vest? When puppies wear their yellow branded Canine Companions® vests, it tells those around them that they are working. The vest has special words on it that say 'future service dog.'

Why is the kennel used? If a puppy is not able to be supervised, they relax in the kennel so they cannot get into mischief! The kennel becomes a puppy's special retreat, and they find comfort being in it.

And finally–

What is a Facility Dog? Facility dogs are expertly trained dogs who partner with a professional and work in a health care, visitation or educational setting.

How long does it take for a Service Dog to be fully trained? It can take anywhere from 18-24 months to become part of a service dog team.

Can I pet a service dog wearing a vest? Service dogs should not be petted or disturbed while they are working—they have a very important job to do! They are part of a team and need to stay focused. The same is true of any dog that you may encounter. You should never pet a dog without asking permission first.

What happens to dogs that do not make it through the program? Dogs that are not able to go into service dog work can become therapy dogs, or cherished family pets. Regardless of the paths our dogs choose, puppy raisers and Canine Companions® are immensely proud of each one of them.

What can I do to help with a puppy like Barley? You can do a lot of things!
- You can become a volunteer puppy raiser.
- You can volunteer with a puppy raiser group near you.
- You can be a puppy sitter for a day.
- You can show your knowledge about service dogs by remembering not to pet a working dog.

And of course you can share Barley's story with your friends!

Canine Companions®

What can a business ask?

"Is the dog a service animal required because of a disability?"

"What work or task has the dog been trained to perform?"

Learn more at canine.org/advocacy

A SERVICE DOG IS MORE THAN A VEST™

Type of Dog	Definition	Access Rights	Training Required	What to Do If the Dog is Misbehaving
Service/Assistance Dog	A dog trained in specific tasks that mitigate the handler's disability.	Permitted with handler in any place the public is allowed.	Extensively trained to perform specific tasks to mitigate effects of handler's disability.	Must be in control at all times and behave in a safe manner. Aggression or continued misconduct can result in the dog's removal under the Americans with Disabilities Act (ADA).
Puppy in Training	A dog that is learning tasks for a handler with a disability or for a program that provides service dogs.	With permission. Rely on goodwill of businesses for access to prepare the puppy for service. Some state laws permit equal access.	In the process of training and socialization to mitigate the effects of disability.	Must be in control at all times and behave in a safe manner. Puppies in training rely on the goodwill of businesses for access, but can be removed.
Facility Dog	A dog trained in specific tasks to work with professionals and their clients in healthcare, visitation or educational settings.	Extensively trained to perform specific tasks to assist professionals to improve client outcomes.	Extensively trained to perform specific tasks to assist professionals to improve client outcomes.	Must be in control at all times and behave in a safe manner. No public access without clients present.
Emotional Support	A dog or other animal whose sole function is to provide comfort or provide emotional support to its owner with a disability.	Only allowed in the owner's home or dormitory as outlined in the Fair Housing Act.	Basic manners expected but none required by law.	No public access.
Therapy Dog	A certified pet that provides comfort in an approved setting.	Only with permission from the approved setting. Vests ONLY worn during approved visits.	Basic obedience and appropriate temperament expected.	No public access.

Acknowledgements

B arley is one of thousands of graduated service dogs since the founding of **Canine Companions®**.

Canine Companions® is leading the service dog industry so that their clients and their dogs can live with greater independence. They provide service dogs to adults and children with disabilities, veterans, and facility dogs to professionals working in healthcare, criminal justice and educational settings.

Since their founding in 1975, their dogs and all follow-up services are provided at no cost to their clients.

Independence shouldn't be limited to those who look or live a certain way. Disability reaches all races, classes and backgrounds, and Canine Companions® will, too. Clients come to Canine Companions® because of their reputation, the quality of their dogs, the experience of their training staff and the desire to lead life with greater independence. They are committed to providing services to all qualified clients.

For additional information on Canine Companions®, please visit: Canine.org

Duke Canine Cognition Center

In Chapter 4, Barley began a program at the Duke Canine Cognition Center and its Puppy Kindergarten program.

The Duke Puppy Kindergarten program is a longitudinal study funded by the National Institute of Health to assess the impact of different rearing strategies on the behavior and cognitive development of assistance dogs. The goal of the program is to increase the supply of assistance dogs and to see more dogs graduate and serve more people.

Each semester, over a hundred Duke undergraduates help raise puppies from Canine Companions® from 8-20 weeks of age. The students also run the puppies through a range of cognitive games that will function as a kind of early aptitude testing, which will be used in the future as early identifiers of puppies who are most likely to graduate as assistance dogs.

Barley came home from his first day of testing wearing an activity monitor as noted in the story. Similar to a sophisticated Fit Bit, they have been used in other small animal studies but never on puppies until Duke's study began around 2019. These monitors are lightweight, non-invasive, and do not have GPS or tracking capability.

Duke's program uses them because they are interested in documenting puppies' developmental activity and sleep patterns. Intense activities, including play, can have beneficial effects on learning in dogs and sleep also has known effects on learning and memory. Since Duke is studying cognitive development in Canine Companions® puppies, they feel it is important to understand the effects of these activities in puppies as they mature.

In this photo, Barley is testing his self control. Puppies are supported to go around the cylinder to get the treat inside. Looks like Barley decided to take a rest!

To learn more about the Duke program, please visit: https://evolutionaryanthropology.duke.edu/dukepuppy-kindergarten

Meet the Author

Margot with service dog, Felix, Feb. 2024

Margot has trained with over 12 dogs during the last 25 years. She has served as a puppy raiser for twelve service dogs as well as worked with therapy dogs. She firmly believes that all dogs have a purpose and that belief has propelled her to volunteer in multiple dog placement programs that service communities.

Barley, Life as a Facility Dog Puppy is her fourth children's story in the series Tails of Dogs Who Help.

- ♥ *Book 1 - Brisco, Life as a Therapy Dog*
- ♥ *Book 2 - Ely, Life as a Service Dog Puppy*
- ♥ *Book 3 - Rocky, Life as a Guide Dog Puppy*

In telling the stories of the many dogs she has raised, she is excited to teach the message of what our dogs can do for us—whether it be through therapy or through service. The author's hope is these books will be a fun way to educate kids about how these dogs become who they are meant to be by telling it through the eyes of the dog.

Margot is based in North Carolina and married with four children. When she's not working with dogs, helping with homework, or volunteering at schools, you can find her hiking, swimming, or playing the drums and dreaming of when her next service dog puppy will arrive.

She is excited to be working on book 5 in her series.

Want to learn more?

Visit Margot's website: dogswhohelp.com

Follow all the Bennett dogs on social media!
    Instagram: @tailsofdogswhohelp
    Facebook: facebook.com/Tails-Of-Dogs-Who-Help

Margot's books available on Amazon:

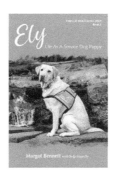

Coming Soon!

The next book in the series:

Tails Of Dogs Who Help
Book 5

Aspen, Life After Rescue

Meet Aspen, a pretty white Lab mix who tells the story of how she finds her true purpose. Follow her journey from being a rescue puppy, to being a member of a growing family, to ultimately becoming a big sister.

In the end, she finds herself in the role of being a friend to many service dog puppies who snuggle their way into her heart.

Coming 2025!

Milton Keynes UK
Ingram Content Group UK Ltd.
UKHW022030150824
446927UK00003B/14